Executive Functioning Skills for Adult ADHD

Proven Tools and Strategies to Strengthen Executive Functioning, Build Healthy Habits, and Overcome ADHD Challenges

Linda Hill & Sarah Davis

Table of Contents

Introduction

ADHD Hasn't changed me… It is me. It's an undeniable and simple fact of who I am.

–Mazey Eddings

If you picked up this book, it's because you have Attention Deficit-Hyperactivity Disorder, or ADHD as we all know it. I want to start off by reassuring you that you are indeed not alone. In fact, I myself have ADHD. This means that I know firsthand how tough it can be living with a brain that functions differently.

I have experienced the paralyzing anxiety that was brought upon me simply because I started to overthink how I will relax on my day off. I've had trouble with forgetting that my friends and family members exist, simply because I didn't have visual reminders of them that I could see on a regular basis. I've experienced time blindness, where I've found myself doom scrolling through social media for an entire day without realizing it. There are so many other symptoms of ADHD that I can go on about. It took me years of researching, experimenting, failing, and trying again, to finally find out how to turn my ADHD into an asset instead of a liability.

Although ADHD is classified as a disorder, I aim to break that stigma. The word disorder is often seen as dirty, meaning that there is something wrong with you. When neurotypical people hear that someone has a mental health disorder, they often believe this person to be unable to function in society, or even pose a danger to society. Of course, this is not true. The only difference is that our brains function in a way that is different from how society perceives normal brain function. Yes, ADHD can make getting into a routine and forming good habits very difficult. It takes so much more out of us to do what others are often able to do without any conscious effort. We are more prone to engaging in behavior that can prohibit us from being productive. This usually leads to us being labeled as "lazy" or "unwilling to focus" by neurotypical people.

This should not discourage you, however. It is still entirely possible for us to form these habits. All we need to do is to gain a better understanding of how ADHD impacts our brain and what that means for how we form habits, as well as how we keep those habits up in our daily lives. That is where this guide comes in. Through this guide, we will gain a better understanding of ADHD, and the science behind it.

We will look into the bad habits we tend to develop, and how to use our ADHD as a tool to break away from these habits and replace them with good habits. We'll focus on the obstacles that are unique to our ADHD minds and explore how we can overcome these obstacles.

Using this workbook, you will not only learn how to develop good habits and a routine, but you will be given the tools to do so. This workbook is specifically designed to work with your ADHD to help you take control of your life and understand yourself and your actions a lot better. Each chapter will include an exercise that is specifically designed to help you systematically gain better control over your ADHD symptoms and by extension your own behavior.

Finally, we will look into the positive impact that good habits can have on your entire life. This includes everything from your mental health, your work, and even your relationships. I'll share some strategies with you that you can use to build resilience and overcome any setbacks you might face. Which unfortunately you will do at some point in your journey.

I want you to remember that ADHD does not automatically mean that you are unable to form good habits, or that you will form bad habits. ADHD does make it more difficult for us to remain in a set routine, it makes it more difficult for us to follow habits that are accepted by society as good, but that does not make you bad in any way. We live in a society that has been made by neurotypicals, for neurotypicals. So, while they may have the advantage when it comes to functioning in what is accepted as the typical way, we tend to have the advantage when it comes to functioning in extraordinary ways.

One such way is that we tend to be more observant, without even realizing it. Have you noticed that you tend to be more empathic than those around you that are neurotypical? Or, perhaps you are able to better identify patterns, or mistakes in patterns than others can. This is a direct result of our brains working differently. Since we struggle to remain focused on one certain thing, our brain starts to pick up on small details around us. This often happens without us realizing it. This is why you will regularly find yourself staring out of a window, or even at a blank space on the wall, without realizing how you got there. While our brains start to take in the small details around us, it processes them and makes us more aware of our surroundings, the body language of people in our vicinity, and so much more. So, without realizing it, we might actually be paying more attention than anyone realizes.

While this can make ADHD function like a superpower, very often the problem we have as people with ADHD is that we are not very well understood, even by ourselves. By educating ourselves on the cause of ADHD, the symptoms, and the strengths, we can make ADHD the strongest tool in our success while also educating those around us. This will help the world to be more accepting of ADHD and could even help us to change society in a way that can make it more accommodating to our ADHD ways.

As I've mentioned before, I also have an ADHD mind, and I've also had to learn about myself and how I work before I was able to increase my productivity. Now, my aim is to help others with ADHD to learn about themselves, and to find out how they can live their lives to their fullest potential.

This book will go beyond just understanding yourself. It will go to understanding how to help yourself to achieve your goals and reach your dreams.

CHAPTER 1

Understanding ADHD and Building Habits

The experience I have had is that once you start talking about [experiencing a mental health struggle], you realize that actually your part of quite a big club.

–Prince Harry

The first step to understanding ADHD and how it affects your habit-building abilities, is to know exactly what ADHD is. Knowledge is one of the most powerful tools in your arsenal and should be encouraged. We tend to fear the things that we do not understand, even when it is an aspect of ourselves. So, to combat that, we need to learn why we have ADHD, why it is extremely important for us to build good habits, and what the most common challenges for us are.

What Is ADHD?

Attention-Deficit/Hyperactivity "Disorder" or ADHD is classified as a mental disorder that affects both children as well as adults. It has been identified as one of the most commonly diagnosed childhood disorders. ADHD is normally diagnosed during childhood and believed to last into adulthood in only two-thirds of cases. However, I am yet to meet someone that was diagnosed with ADHD as a child and does not still have it as an adult.

Our understanding of ADHD is ever changing, and still relatively in its infant stages. The information that we believed to have been correct 20 years ago is now being called into question. This is because our understanding of ADHD is always improving, and assumptions that we made in the past now need to be proven. For example, ADHD and ADD (Attention Deficit Disorder) were seen as separate disorders. Recently, however, it has become understood that ADD and ADHD are the exact same disorder. Someone with ADHD might present as hyperactive in the morning, but by the afternoon they might be more dissociative instead which was traditionally seen as a symptom of ADD.

ADHD is normally diagnosed when certain symptoms have been found to be recurring for the majority of your life and impacts all aspects of your life. However, almost every single person will experience ADHD-like symptoms at some point in their lives. That is why the key factor is that these symptoms must have been present from childhood. The symptoms that normally point to ADHD are:

- Impulsivity.

- Difficulty prioritizing/disorganization.

- Difficulty with time management.

- Difficulty focusing on a single task.

- Difficulty in multitasking.

- Difficulty in planning.

- Difficulty in seeing tasks through to completion.

- Excessive restlessness.

- Low tolerance to frustration.

- Low tolerance to stress.

- Frequent mood changers.

- Short temper.

Statistically, we see that around 8.4% of all children (Danielson et al., 2018) and 2.5% of all adults (Simon et al., 2009) are affected by ADHD. Additionally, boys are more commonly diagnosed with ADHD and diagnosed at a younger age than girls. This is supposedly due to the fact girls tend to present as inattentive, while boys tend to present as hyperactive, as well as that girls tend to internalize their symptoms, and boys tend to externalize theirs. However, there is still some evidence to show that there is a bias in treatment referrals, and even in the use of medication when it comes to girls (Quinn & Madhoo, 2014).

The truly remarkable thing about ADHD is that nobody really understands the cause behind it. Research into this condition has linked it to genetics, brain structure, and environmental influences. This leads to the obvious conclusion, that anyone can be diagnosed with ADHD. That being said, you are more prone to being at risk for ADHD if you have a direct family member that has ADHD or another mental health disorder, your mother used substances such as tobacco, alcohol, or drugs during pregnancy, you were born premature, or were exposed to toxins such as lead during childhood.

The way that ADHD works is that your brain is literally structured differently. If you have ADHD, it means that there are lower levels of certain chemicals such as dopamine and norepinephrine in your brain. Your brain uses these chemicals to stimulate certain areas and transmit signals between nerve cells. The areas that are stimulated with these chemicals are the areas of your brain that are used for your executive functions, such as your working memory, problem-solving skills, emotional control, and several others.

That is why ADHD medication tends to stimulate people that do not have ADHD, while they simply assist in making those with ADHD perform in a typical manner. The secret here is that the stimulants that you take tend to force your body and brain to create enough of the chemicals you lack, in order to allow your brain to work in a typical fashion. That is one of the reasons why addictive substances are so much more addictive to people with ADHD. It helps you to function in a neurotypical way, a way that you have been told your whole life you should be like. This is also why people with ADHD tend to react differently to stimulants such as caffeine than neurotypical people do. When a neurotypical person has their cup of coffee in the morning, their brains are flooded with an elevated amount of the chemicals that stimulate their executive functioning. When we have our cup of coffee, our brain receives more of the chemicals that we lack, which causes our executive functioning center to work as it is supposed to. Which in turn makes us more relaxed, focused, and calmer in general.

If you have not been diagnosed with ADHD but suspect that you might have ADHD, I suggest you see a mental health practitioner capable of making such a diagnosis immediately. Unfortunately, our understanding of ADHD and the subsequent diagnosis of it is still a fairly young science. This means that many people that do actually have ADHD have been branded as *gifted* or *problematic* in the past, but when looked at with the new information at our disposal, we make the correct diagnosis.

Importance of Building Good Habits

We all know that building good habits are important to

everyone, but it is more so for those of us that have ADHD. By forming good habits, you combat the challenges that are brought on by ADHD. Positive habits and a productive routine can help you to improve your executive functioning where your ADHD may be causing challenges.

By following the same habit of waking up every morning at 6 a.m., going for a run around the block, and then showering and going to work, we don't have to worry about planning our mornings or managing our time in getting ready each day. All we have to do is to get into the habit of following this routine to ensure that we have a positive impact on our health and productivity levels. The concept remains the same for whatever habits you decide to implement in your life. You no longer need to make a conscious daily decision regarding when you need to take a shower, when to exercise, or even what time to leave for work. By planning your time to wake up and getting into the habit of repeating certain tasks in a certain order, your executive functions become habits that are followed, instead of tasks that need to be done every day.

Additionally, if you want to change your habits to be more productive in your daily life, it is suggested that instead of aiming to immediately rid yourself of negative or bad habits, you instead focus on adding positive habits as a start. As you add more of these good habits, you will automatically start to change and remove the bad habits from your life. For example, if you find that your ADHD often makes it difficult for you to get out of bed and start your day, a challenge that has become all too real for those of us that work from home, getting into the habit of exercising in the mornings can help you to get out of the habit of sleeping in.

This will in turn improve your focus and productivity. Maintaining Focus is another activity that is impaired and made more difficult by an ADHD mind. However, by getting into the habit of breaking your tasks into smaller steps and completing only these certain tasks at certain times, you reduce the cognitive load that your mind requires to start focusing and remain focused. Very often we try to force ourselves to focus on getting the dishes washed, instead of becoming distracted by something else.

For this example, I'll make up a little scenario for you. Let's say we have a woman called Mary who wants to remain more focused on completing her tasks at work. She works in an open office and her tasks usually include capturing financial data. Looking up and down from numbers the whole day does not stimulate her a lot, and she often finds herself getting distracted by what her coworkers are doing, and even more so when she can hear their conversations. If Mary starts to get into the habit of capturing her clients' financials first thing in the mornings when she gets in and taking a coffee break with a coworker only when she has done a certain amount of work, then she will increase her productivity, and help herself stay focused for longer. The way this works isn't that Mary starts to ignore everything and everyone around her. Instead, she enforces a habit of rewarding herself for maintaining focus. She motivates herself by saying "If I capture 200 receipts, I can have a coffee with Jane."

This will all mean that your day-to-day life becomes more consistent, which in turn allows you to better follow through in completing tasks. When you become used to repeating the same good habits, it is almost as if your mind switches into auto-pilot mode when you do these tasks. When you don't have to think of doing the task, it becomes easier to complete.

An easy task to complete also means that you will be faster and more efficient at completing this task. When paired with the auto-pilot idea that a good habit eventually offers you, you will reap the benefits when it comes to your time management skills. When I first started implementing habits and a schedule, I had a set schedule. I would wake up at 8 a.m., have coffee, and be in the shower by 8:15 a.m. At 9 a.m. I would start working and at 10 a.m. an alarm would go off telling me to stretch my legs, make another cup of coffee, and just walk outside and breathe fresh air for a few seconds. After a while of following this schedule, my productivity did not only increase, but I also found myself getting up seconds before my 10 a.m. alarm goes off every morning. My body and mind got into the habit of following this routine to such an extent, that before I knew it, I had been doing it without thinking or needing an alarm.

This made me a lot less impulsive and helped me to develop

better self-regulation skills. I was no longer as easily distracted by scrolling through my phone or packing away my laundry so that I could do the dishes, in order to work.

Eventually, I found this routine helped to also regulate my emotional well-being. The paralyzing anxiety of not knowing what to do, or where to start had begun to fade. The stress from not completing tasks in a timely manner dissipated since I could now complete my tasks on time, and the depression from not getting to everything I wanted to do in a single day also started to fade away.

At the end of the day, building good habits allows you to minimize the negative impact that ADHD has on your everyday life.

Common Challenges People With ADHD Face When Building Habits

I want you to note that these challenges that we need to overcome in order to build new habits are also the same areas in which we will improve our lives with good habits.

This is a paradox. We need to overcome a challenge, to be able to better overcome that exact challenge. It will take hard work and dedication, but it can be done.

An ADHD mind needs to constantly be stimulated. When we

do not receive enough stimulation, our mind easily wanders in search of more stimulating input. This becomes especially more common when we engage in repetitive tasks. Such as following a routine.

This is also why we are often very inconsistent. The first time we do something, it is new and exciting. But when we are asked to repeat that activity or action, we are no longer interested because we've done it already.

That is when our impulse control challenges kick in. While in search of more stimuli, we end up acting impulsively to find them. We may be so bored with making a candle every day at 2:15 p.m. that while making the candle, we start to clean the candle-making equipment instead.

This lack of stimuli causes a lack of focus on one task. When our mind then wanders to another task that actually stimulates us, we become completely absorbed by that task and tend to hyper focus on it. Of course, being extremely focused can be a good thing. However, we tend to focus so much on this new and often irrelevant task, that we completely forget about everything else.

This is why we find it so difficult to plan and to stick to those plans. When we try to break activities and tasks down into smaller, more manageable tasks, we often find that it is difficult to think of only one small step in the process, and we automatically gravitate back towards the bigger picture.

This is where our emotional factors come into play. An ADHD mind has greater difficulty with regulating emotions. This means that when we look at the bigger picture it is easier for us to become overwhelmed or demotivated. When we are in a negative frame of mind this is even more likely to happen. I often find myself unable to wash one dish when I am in a bad mood because washing one dish means that I need to clean the entire kitchen, which in turn feels so overwhelming and exhausting before I even begin. This results in the dishes heaping up and becoming a bigger task than they would have been if I had washed the one dish as soon as I used it, and in turn this big pile of dishes makes me feel more overwhelmed, which makes me more depressed.

People with ADHD also tend to have difficulties with balancing their work and personal life. Most often we tend to feel overwhelmed with both and end up either fixating on being too perfect at work or so stressed out that we rather procrastinate. Both of these can end up negatively impacting your productivity levels. Aside from this, you might also end up fixating on your work, which can cause you to keep thinking about work, and even feeling guilty when you are not busy working.

The next challenge we face is remaining focused, while there are possible distractions around. This is a challenge that tends to impact us more as children since we are more capable of reminding ourselves to focus when we are adults. This does not mean that remaining focused will be easy though. The slightest noise or movement in our vicinity could end up distracting us. Aside from being distracted, too much input in the form of noise or movement can make us feel overstimulated as well.

On the opposite side of the coin, we have a tendency to become hyper focused on certain tasks. This is when we feel like we're in our element and super fixated on a task. While this does sound like a good thing, and it can be used as a powerful tool, it also has its dark side as it is difficult to choose the object of our hyper fixation. So, while we might try to make our work, or exercise our hyper fixation, we might find ourselves hyper focusing on the history of the lightbulb instead.

Another obstacle we tend to face is our mind being extremely active. This could lead to problems such as being restless, or insomnia. When was the last time you found yourself being able to focus solely on the subject of a meeting? This is because your mind is racing and thinking of a million other things, and could even lead to anxiety and panic attacks.

It is often exactly this problem we have with our minds being far too active that leads us to feel overwhelmed. Unfortunately, as I've mentioned, when we feel overwhelmed we tend to procrastinate even more and focus on unimportant tasks that distract us from whatever is making us feel overwhelmed. This in turn usually causes us to take even longer to complete our stress-inducing tasks, which naturally causes more stress. Eventually, you may experience burnout symptoms and exhaustion.

ADHD also has a long history of being linked to eating disorders. This is because when we become distracted or hyper focused, we might fall into what is called time blindness. This is when we completely lose track of time and by extension the other tasks that are important to our health, such as eating. When we then remember our nutritional needs, we end up overeating to compensate for the meals we missed.

Another challenge brought upon us by our tendency of becoming distracted is that we might become bored more easily. This is because when we find a task to not be very interesting to us, our attention wanders away from this task. Which of course, leads us to feeling bored with the task at hand.

When you put all of these challenges that we tend to face together, it should come as no surprise that we also suffer from low self-esteem. This is of course, not just due to the other challenges that we face, but also partly based on the fact that people with ADHD are often very misunderstood. At a young age, we are usually filled with so much energy that we are seen as a nuisance to those around us, and we eventually become so bored with all the excess energy, that we might engage in activity that is seen as misbehaving. When we are constantly criticized for this by others, and we find ourselves feeling ashamed of our ADHD symptoms, low self-esteem is almost guaranteed.

Exercise

The first step into obtaining and following good habits is to understand what you want to achieve with these habits, and what stops you from doing so at this moment. To do this we'll fill in the below sheet, I've done an example for you to more easily see what I mean.

Example

What habits do I want to build?	I want to create a consistent daily work routine.
Why do you want to build this habit?	To feel more productive at work. To feel less stressed overall. To get a promotion. To have more free time over weekends. To feel more stable.
What is making this difficult?	I have trouble repeating the same action daily. I have trouble waking up at the

	same time every morning.
	I often get overwhelmed with my work.
	I tend to lose focus on tasks that feel repetitive.
	New tasks scare me and cause me to procrastinate.
	I often get interrupted making a schedule and keeping focus more difficult.
	I feel unappreciated in my work.
	I am bored at work.
	I work from home and tend to get back in bed during my breaks.
	My dogs are constantly running and barking which distracts me.
	When it's too quiet I cannot focus.
How do you feel your ADHD impacts your	My ADHD makes it hard to

ability to build this habit?	focus. My ADHD affects my mood negatively. My ADHD makes me feel either overstimulated or under-stimulated.
What factors aside from your ADHD make these habits difficult?	I have a lot of outside distractions and influences that take my attention away from my work.
What strategies have you tried to help you build this habit so far?	I have set alarms at the same time every day. I have turned my phone off.

Your Turn

What habits do I want to build?	
Why do you want to build this habit?	
What is making this difficult?	

How do you feel your ADHD impacts your ability to build this habit?	
What factors aside from your ADHD make these habits difficult?	
What strategies have you tried to help you build this habit so far?	

CHAPTER 2

Identifying and Setting Goals

People with goals succeed because they know where they're going.
–Earl Nightingale

When building habits, we need to understand what we want to achieve through these habits. That is where our goals come in. We need to understand what we want to accomplish in order to accomplish it. To determine what we want is to identify our goals. To determine which of these goals we plan on reaching is to set our goals.

Why Is Setting Goals So Important?

By setting clear and specific goals, you are giving yourself a clear direction to follow, and something to focus on. It also helps to add a purpose to your new habits. You are now forming good habits for a reason that you can identify with, instead of just forming a habit because that is what you were told to do.

When you have a goal that you truly want to achieve you will be more inclined to put your energy into this goal. You will be more motivated to achieve this goal, due to the fact that it now has a purpose that is important to you. This makes the process of building a new habit not only more engaging but also more rewarding since it will feel so much better when you achieve your goal.

You also now have a way of measuring your progress. Goals can be broken down into smaller, more achievable steps. Let's say for example your goal is to wake up at a certain time every day, you can measure your progress toward your goal by adding milestones. Such as waking up at the correct time one day, then three days in a row, then a week, a month, and then three months. And before you realize it you achieve your goal, but you also have milestones that you could celebrate and measure your progress with while working towards your goal.

This is especially important to people with ADHD as this helps you to maintain focus, release dopamine, and give you something new to work on, instead of making you feel like you are repeating the same task over, and over. Remember that dopamine is one of the chemicals in our brain that we lack, and by celebrating our accomplishments and making ourselves feel good, we cause our brains to create more dopamine, which in turn helps us to function more typically.

By setting smaller goals that help us to achieve our larger goal we also help ourselves to get into the habit of good habits and a constant routine. Since this is something that is difficult for us, we can make it easier by tricking our brains into creating dopamine when we do it, so that we cause our ADHD to crave these goals and milestones even more.

The same idea can be used to help increase our time management. If we allow ourselves to celebrate successful time management, our brain becomes used to creating the dopamine we lack whenever we do. Which in turn makes time management even better and easier.

Goals also allow us to keep ourselves accountable. If we set shorter and more achievable goals that we plan on achieving, then we also know when we do not achieve these goals. Now while this might sound like a bad thing, it is also an opportunity for us. When we miss our smaller goals, we can rely on our support systems to help motivate us and look into what caused us to miss this milestone. We can then identify the problem and have someone help us to overcome it.

Setting goals is the key to succeeding in improving our quality of life. It is how we motivate ourselves, keep track of our progress, identify our weak points, and even achieve our eventual success.

Goal Setting Strategy

To ensure that you will achieve your goals, you will need to set your goals up to be successful. Remember, the key to success is planning for it. This can easily be achieved by using the SMART goals framework.

Specific

The S in SMART means creating very specific goals. Instead of saying that you want to keep your house clean, your goal should be more focused, such as wanting to wash the dishes every day, and mop the floors twice a day. This allows you to ensure that you know what your goal is, and how to achieve it. If your goal is too vague, it's easy to lose track of it.

Measurable

A specific and measurable goal means that you know exactly when you have achieved your goal. You don't have to wonder if your house is clean enough, you will know whether you have reached all your goals for a clean house, or not.

Achievable

When you set a goal for yourself, it should be something that is within your power. Setting a goal like I want my house to never get dirty, is an unachievable goal. There is no way in life that anyone can achieve that goal. In the same sense saying you want to clean the house top to bottom every day is also an unachievable goal, as the chances are that you do not have the time or for that matter, the need to do so.

Relevant

We've already covered this quite a bit, but your goals should be relevant to you. If you were to make a goal of writing 5000 words every day, the goal might not be relevant to you, but it is relevant to me. This means that I would be a lot more motivated to achieve this goal than you would be.

Time-Bound

Everything in our lives has a deadline. That project at work needs to be done at a designated time and day. We need to have dinner ready at a certain time. The same thing is true for our goals. When we give our goals a time frame, we give ourselves not only more motivation to ensure we stick with it, we also add another aspect of measurability to our goals.

Turning Your Goals Into Smaller Achievable Steps

The next step in creating achievable goals is breaking down your goals. If we keep using the home cleaning example, we would have taken it from in general just cleaning the house, all the way to completing certain tasks that ensure that your house is cleaned every day. These tasks will now be broken down into individual steps.

By breaking your tasks into steps, you give yourself a to-do list. You make a plan on how to achieve your goals, which allows you to focus on the here and now. Instead of looking at a mountain of dishes that need to be done, while there are still several other tasks that need to be done (which for those of us with ADHD will often cause us to start several different tasks but complete none) you instead focus on just one step. The dishes need to be collected from the entire house. That is all you need to do in order to be closer to your goal.

When you look at any task that leads you to your goal, break down the task. Make sure you can see each and every step that will lead to the completion of the task. These steps can be as simple as waking up at a certain time or doing a specific action for a specific amount of time.

Every small step you take is an achievement, you are working to complete your goals. This helps you to maintain your focus on the here and now. It allows you to measure your progress. It even gives you an opportunity to celebrate your progress.

Exercise

We need to turn what we have learned into something that we can use. By now you should have a greater goal in mind. Something vague like being more productive at work. You should understand why you want to achieve this goal, and what the challenges are in achieving these goals. Now we need to break down our goals and be sure that they are well thought out and understood.

Example

What is your goal?	Clean the house every day.
Break your goal into tasks	1. Do the dishes each day
	2. Sweep/vacuum every day
	3. Make the bed each day
	4. Mop the floors every second day

Break your tasks into smaller steps.	1. Dishes
	
	a. Collect dishes from every room in the house.
	
	b. Pack dishes neatly on the counter.
	
	c. Wash dishes in order;
	
	    i. Glasses and cups
	
	    ii. Cutlery
	
	    iii. Plates and bowls

iv.   Cookware

d. Dry and pack away dishes in reverse order.

e. Clean washing basin.

2. Sweep/vacuum

a. Vacuum bedroom carpets.

b. Sweep the bathroom floor towards the hallway.

c. Sweep the hallway into the living room.

d. Sweep the kitchen into the living room.

e. Sweep the living room towards the front door.

f. Collect all dirt in a dustpan and throw it out in the outside bin.

g. Vacuum rugs in the living room.

3. Making the bed

	a. Remove blankets from...	
Set time frames for your goal.	Daily:	Complete tasks every evening before bed
	Weekly:	Complete daily tasks at least six days per week.
	Monthly:	Achieve weekly goals for three consecutive months.
	Yearly:	Achieve goal for one year without fail
	End Goal:	Get into the habit of achieving daily tasks without needing tracking or reminders.

Your Turn

You can use this template for any goals you have. You can create a similar one or print this one out as many times as needed for all your goals.

What is your goal?	
Break your goal into tasks	1.
	2.
	3.
	4.
	5.
	6.
	7.
	8.

	9.
	10.
Break your tasks into smaller steps.	

Set time frames for your goal.	Daily:	
	Weekly:	
	Monthly:	
	Yearly:	
	End Goal:	

CHAPTER 3

Creating A Daily Routine

We are what we repeatedly do
—**Aristotle**

Now that you have established what your goals are, and what the exact steps are in achieving these goals, you need to use these goals to create your personal daily routine. Of course, this is something that is unique to each of us. Not one single person lives a life that is exactly like that of another person. This means that I can advise you as much as I want to, but I will never be able to give you a predetermined plan that will suit all your needs. This is why it is important that you understand how to create your own effective daily routine.

Benefits of Establishing a Daily Routine

Establishing a daily routine is perhaps the most important part of developing good habits. These are the building blocks of habits. Your daily routine is the practice of your habits.

However, daily routines are intentional whereas habits are unintentional behavior, developed through conscious effort.

This also means that having a daily routine has some benefits that differ from those of good habits. The first of the benefits we will look into is the improvement of your mental health. A stable and constant routine has been found to assist in addiction recovery, mood disorders, and a whole list of other mental health problems.

One of the reasons for this is the reduced stress levels that you experience with a daily routine. This happens when you get used to your routine and know what to expect from your daily life. When you know what is going to happen, when you are going to eat, when you are going to work, when you are taking a break, your mind can rest.

Your mental health is not the only aspect of your health that will benefit you. Your general health overall will also improve. This is because you will eat more regularly than if you do not have a routine. If you have added exercise into your routine as well, that is even more health benefits that you will enjoy.

Of course, with all these health benefits, you will start feeling better. You will have your day planned out and have more energy and motivation for your day. This will cause an increase in your productivity levels. This is due to your improved time management abilities and the fact that you no longer have to choose and think about your day and actions, but rather focus on the task at hand.

Tips for Creating an Individual Routine

As I've already mentioned, each and every person lives their own life differently. This means that we need to create routines that are specially tailored to us as individuals. To do so we need to look at all the factors that influence our lives.

You will need to take into consideration the external factors of your life. These would be factors like whether you have a set time that you need to work. Whether you have any responsibilities that you need to adapt your routine to.

You will then also need to look into yourself. What are the internal factors that affect you? These are factors such as whether you are an early riser, a late sleeper, a night owl, or a day person. This will determine what works better for you. For example, I personally work better at night, and I'm a late sleeper, but I have responsibilities early mornings. This means that for me it is easier to shower before going to bed at night so that I can sleep as late as possible in the morning. This allows me to work at night when I do my best work, get enough sleep, and wake up at a time that is comfortable for me.

You will need to assess yourself and determine what works best for you. I also want you to remember that if your individual routine is different from what society deems normal, it is entirely okay.

All this means that you should also be sure that your routine is flexible enough that it can be adjusted and made to fit your lifestyle as it changes. This also means that you should continuously track and evaluate your daily routines. By keeping an eye on your routine and determining what is working, and changing what is not working, you can maximize the benefits that you will enjoy from this daily routine.

Lastly, to help ensure that you remain in the practice of following your routine every day at the same time, remember to set alarms and timers for yourself. These reminders will help ensure that you stick to your routine and improve your time management. You don't have to constantly check time or remember when you have to perform certain tasks. Your phone or smart assistant will be able to do so.

Common Reasons Why Routines Fail

ADHD symptoms are quite similar in all of us that have ADHD, as are the challenges and setbacks we face. This also means that the reasons for our routines failing will also be similar. Luckily, when we know what these reasons are, we can plan for them, and identify them when we face them.

One of the first reasons why our routines might fail is that we might become bored with our routine. This is natural for people with ADHD, as we don't like repetition much. This is also why it is important for us to ensure that we schedule fun activities into our routines that ensure we don't easily become bored with our routine. You can also change up your routine once in a while, especially if you start to notice that you are getting bored with it.

When you create your routine, also be sure that you keep it somewhat flexible, as a rigid routine can also make you feel overwhelmed, trapped, or even bored, leading to another common reason for failing in your routine. Remember that your routine is there to help you, not to limit you.

You also need to be on the lookout that your routine does not start to feel overwhelming to you. This is usually easily spotted as you might wake up in the mornings and immediately start going through the routine in your mind while feeling negative about the tasks that lay before you. This is also when you tend to start procrastinating a bit more, or hardly get out of bed at all.

Another danger to your routine is distractions and interruptions. Regardless of how determined you are to follow your routine, any small distraction such as your phone receiving a notification, or an interruption like someone starting to talk to you, can lead to a major disruption in your routine. When your routine and plans have been thrown for a loop, you require your executive functioning skills to get yourself back on track, and of course, as we know, our ADHD makes that a rather difficult task.

Of course, there are other ways that our ADHD can lead to disruptions in our routines. When we become hyper focused on a certain task, or dissociative and distracted while attempting to finish a task, our ADHD could start to run rampant. This is when we get in the way of our own routines. This is also perhaps the reason that most of our routines fail, as this reason is the most frequent to affect us, and the most rooted in our ADHD diagnosis.

The final reason we have that our routines tend to fail is that we lose the motivation needed to follow our routines. This is normally because our goals feel too far removed, or we lost sight of them. It might also occur after we suffered some other type of failure or setback, where our goals might feel too difficult to accomplish.

While these are not the only reasons why we could fail in following a routine, they are the most common causes for people with ADHD. It's important that we know what obstacles could stand in our way and understand that even if these obstacles get the better of us, it does not mean that we will never succeed. We would never have known that these are the most common reasons for us to suffer setbacks if these setbacks did not happen to all of us.

Strategies for Overcoming Setbacks

A setback is one of the guarantees in creating a daily routine. It is something you will face at some point. This might be discouraging, but to achieve your goals you need to work through it. Learning to overcome your setbacks is essential to ensuring your success.

The first step in learning to overcome setbacks is by embracing a growth mindset. This allows you to accept that setbacks will occur and that they are not signs of failures but instead, opportunities to succeed. When you suffer a setback, you have the opportunity to identify what went wrong and improve on your method.

To do this you need to be compassionate towards yourself. Understand that this is normal. You are a human being, and you will fall along the road. Do not allow these setbacks to let you talk down to yourself. It is okay and you did nothing wrong. Build yourself up and forgive yourself.

When you have forgiven yourself, you can start to analyze your setbacks. Remove yourself from the situation and look at it objectively. Why did this setback occur? Was it from external factors, a problem in your plan, were your expectations set too high? You need to identify the root of the setback and determine what you can do to change this in the future.

When you have identified what the cause of your setback is, you need to identify what changes you can implement to ensure that you never face the same setbacks again, and then do so. You might need to change your schedule a bit, reassess your goal, or find more support. By adjusting your approach, you plan for future setbacks.

Although you may do all this, it can still be difficult to power through these setbacks alone. This is why having a support system. When you fail to be kind to yourself, or you cannot figure out how to change your approach or what the root of your setback is, it helps to talk to someone. It can be a friend or a family member, in fact I suggest multiple of each. They are there to be kind to you and assure you of your confidence and capabilities. They can offer a new perspective on your challenges and your approach to overcoming challenges. They are there to help you when you struggle to help yourself.

There will also be times when you start to feel overwhelmed. It will be hard to recover from some setbacks, and at times you will feel as if you are treading through waist-high mud. You will feel as if you put in all your time and effort and see no progress. When this occurs, you need to take a breath. Focus on the steps in each task and keep your focus on it. Make sure you break down each step, each goal, and each aspect of your life as much as possible. Don't forget to break your achievements down as well.

When you break your achievements down as well, you have the opportunity to celebrate each achievement. This will not only help you to keep track of your progress but allow you to celebrate your progress. By celebrating as much of your progress as possible, you will force your body to create the good chemicals that it needs to function in a neurotypical way. It also helps to litter your journey with good memories. Which means when you think back onto your journey, it will be a happy one. This will help to keep you motivated throughout your journey.

Exercise

Below I'll give you an example for a daily routine schedule. After that I will give you a few pre-made templates that can be used and adjusted to your specific needs. I will also give you an empty template that allows you full freedom.

Example

Morning	
07:30	Wake up.
08:00	Morning hygiene routine.
08:30	Have breakfast.

Work Time	
09:00	Go to work.
09:15	Start working day.
10:30	Break for 15 minutes
10:45	Focus on work for 1 hour 15 minutes.
12:00	30 minutes lunch.
12:30	Mid-day meditation.
13:00	Focus on work for 1 hour 15 minutes.
14:15	15-minute break
14:30	Focus on work for 1 hour 15 minutes.
15:45	Start packing up.

Evening	
16:00	Go home.
16:15	Start dinner.
17:30	Eat dinner.
18:00	Do dishes
18:30	Clean floors
19:00	Watch TV/ Relax
21:00	Work on a hobby.
23:00	Evening hygiene routine.
00:00	Go to bed.

Your Turn

Blank Template

Morning	
__:__	
__:__	
__:__	
__:__	
__:__	
Work Time	
__:__	
__:__	
__:__	

__:__	
__:__	
__:__	
__:__	
__:__	
__:__	
__:__	

Evening

__:__	
__:__	
__:__	
__:__	

__:__	
__:__	
__:__	
__:__	
__:__	

Fitness Template

Morning	
07:00	Wake up
07:15	Jog for 20 minutes
07:35	Start morning hygiene routine.
__:__	
__:__	

Work Time	
__:__	
__:__	
__:__	
__:__	
__:__	
__:__	
__:__	
__:__	
__:__	
__:__	

Evening	
16:00	Leave work and go home.
16:30	Do push-ups
16:40	Do sit-ups
16:50	Jog for 10 minutes
17:00	Start evening hygiene routine
__:__	
__:__	
__:__	
__:__	

Healthy Eating Template

Morning	
07:00	Wake up
07:15	Have full breakfast
07:45	Start morning hygiene routine.
__:__	
__:__	
Work Time	
__:__	
__:__	
__:__	
__:__	

12:00	Eat a full lunch.
__:__	
__:__	
__:__	
__:__	
__:__	
Evening	
16:00	Leave work and go home.
16:15	Prepare dinner and have dinner
17:30	Do prep work for next day's breakfast and lunch
18:30	Do dishes

__:__	
__:__	
__:__	
__:__	
__:__	

CHAPTER 4

Implementing Healthy Habits

If you are going to achieve excellence in big things, you develop the habit in little matters. Excellence is not an exception, it is a prevailing attitude.
–Colin Powell

Now that we've looked into creating routines we need to look into how we can turn those routines into healthy habits and ensure that these habits remain with us. For people that have ADHD, this is not the easiest accomplishment as we tend to lose habits very quickly.

Strategies for Building Healthy Habits

The entire purpose of building a daily routine and identifying and setting goals for ourselves is to create healthy habits. These habits are meant to help us function better in life. For that reason, we'll need a few strategies to ensure that we successfully build these habits.

The first bit of advice I can give you in creating healthy habits is to start small. Don't try to create a habit that will drastically alter your life. If the change is too big all at once, it is more difficult to adapt to it. Instead, by getting into smaller habits, such as eating more vegetables, taking short walks every day, and other little habits that will improve your life, without turning it upside down.

Of course, these habits need to align with the goals that you have set. You need to ensure that the habits you create are attuned to these goals and will assist you in reaching these goals. For example, if your goal is to exercise more regularly, then the habit should be to go on a daily run for example.

As we've already established, these habits are formed through repeating a daily routine. Remember that the difference between a routine and a habit is that your routine is done on purpose and planned out, whereas habits are positive and good actions that you get so used to repeating that you do it without thinking.

This is most likely to happen when you repeatedly do activities that you enjoy and that releases dopamine. This is especially helpful for those of us with ADHD. By completing activities that we enjoy as part of our daily routines, our mind releases the chemicals that we need to function in a typical way. This helps us to function in a typical way. So, when we enjoy our daily activities they are far more likely to become habits for us. To find these enjoyable activities, you will need to try out different ones. Keep in mind that not all activities that align with your goals will be enjoyable, but you might be able to make them enjoyable.

For example, doing the dishes will most probably not be enjoyable for you. However, by adding music to the task or making a game out of it, you can easily turn it into an enjoyable activity that works with your ADHD instead of against it.

If your desired habits include healthy eating habits, there are some adjustments that you can make to build better eating habits as well. These are habits like preparing your meals in advance and stocking your kitchen with more healthy foods than junk food so that even if you are in the mood for a quick snack, you opt for a healthier one instead of junk food. Another trick is to plan your food and snacks for the entire week in advance. This is another trick to help take the choice out of the equation in the moment so that you can combat your impulsive behavior.

Another strategy to get yourself into the habit of eating better is to practice what is called mindful eating. This is when you slow down the speed at which you eat and focus more on the signals that your body gives you to inform you when you are hungry, when you are full, and when you are only eating as a form of stimulation.

Just like with your daily routine, you can also lean on your support system for both support and accountability in creating healthy habits. A very effective way of using your support system to help you in an ethical and mutually beneficial way is to work together with your friends to develop habits together that are beneficial to both of you. When someone has the same goals as you, they are more effective at being motivational and holding you accountable. They might also be more empathic as they will most likely face similar challenges as you on this journey.

This will also allow you to more easily track and compare your progress. Tracking your progress on habits is a bit different from tracking your progress on activities though. By directly tracking your progress daily, you are making your habits a conscious effort that makes it more of a daily routine, than a subconscious habit. Instead, your habits are better tracked at weekly and monthly intervals, to see if you remember participating in them and then adjusting your approach to ensure that you are more prone to participate in these activities.

To improve your body's production of dopamine and increase your chances of successfully developing these new habits, you should remember to reward yourself for your success as well. This will be similar to when you reward yourself for achieving your daily routine goals, however, it would happen less frequently. So, don't be afraid of making these rewards bigger and more enjoyable.

To improve your chances of achieving good habits in regard to productivity and exercise, quality sleep is important. Remember that you should adapt your sleeping schedule to suit your personal needs and accommodate your schedule. This includes taking a break from screen time before bedtime since your phone will stimulate your mind and your ADHD will flare up. If you find yourself having difficulty falling asleep at night you can try adding activities such as meditation before bedtime into your daily routine.

Creating positive habits that help to improve your quality of life takes repetition, time, and effort. You will need to continuously assess your success and efforts to ensure that you are adjusting your lifestyle to ensure you promote these healthy habits.

Tips for Making Habits Stick

Once you have begun forming new habits, you need to reinforce these habits. Unfortunately, habits don't just remain with us indefinitely. Especially not good habits. To ensure that your good habits don't slip away, here are a few tips that will help you to ensure they stick.

Firstly, don't become over-ambitious. This is something that we with ADHD tend to struggle with. When we find something new to focus on we can easily become swept up in the excitement and dopamine rush that is induced by the sudden stimulation. However, after the initial focus wears off, we can just as easily feel overwhelmed by the goals and targets we have set for ourselves.

To combat this, we need to concentrate on forming only one habit at a time. You might have goals of improving your eating habits, your productivity at work, your ability to complete mundane chores, and your exercise routine. Instead of cramming your daily routine as full as possible by trying to work on all these aspects at the same time, focus on one at a time instead. Once you have managed to achieve one goal and use it to form healthy habits, you can focus on the next habit you wish to form.

Remember that with each habit you form, you need to keep a close eye on all the previous habits you have formed to make sure that none of them are slipping away either.

While you are forming new habits, having clear visible reminders of your habits will help you to stay focused and keep track of your progress. Although a habit is an action performed without having to think of it, having general reminders of keeping positive habits up, can only help you.

Your habit is ingrained through your daily routine and finding small and consistent reminders in your everyday life that you can link to the activities that you want to become habits will help you to make the shift from purposeful activities into natural habits. These can be triggers such as having dinner while watching the evening news or taking a break at work every day after contacting a specific customer.

Your body will eventually associate these two actions with each other. When this happens, you will no longer need to actively remind yourself to follow through on these habits, as your body will start to crave these habits when it encounters the trigger.

This can also help you to not only remain consistent which as we've already covered is important in forming habits, but to also overcome possible challenges before you need to face them. In the next chapter, we will look more closely at the possible challenges and obstacles, as well as further ways that we can plan and overcome them.

Remember, building habits takes time, patience, and perseverance. Be kind to yourself, expect some setbacks along the way, and maintain a positive mindset. With consistent effort and the right strategies, you can make habits stick and experience positive changes in your life.

The Importance of Self-Care in Maintaining Healthy Habits and Managing ADHD Symptoms

If you have trouble with self-care, I do suggest making your first goal of getting into the habit of practicing self-care. Self-care can help you to mitigate the negative impact that ADHD might have on you, as well as help your mental health in a variety of other ways. This in turn ensures that you have the best chance of achieving success in your future habit formations.

This is due to the fact that proper self-care carries a wide variety of benefits that not only help you to form and keep good habits but also help you to better work with your ADHD as well.

Physical exercise is one of the best forms of self-care for people with ADHD. Not only because it improves your physical health, but also because it causes your body to release endorphins. These are the chemicals that our brains have difficulty with, which means that after regular exercise you will function in a more neuro-typical manner. The endorphins will also help to reduce stress and improve your mood in the long term.

Stress is a big factor for those of us with ADHD. We tend to be affected by stress a lot more severely than others. This is because stress impacts your organizational skills, time management, and impulse control, all aspects of life already impacted by your ADHD. This is one of the dark spiraling circles that ADHD often sends us into. You start experiencing only a small amount of stress and before you know it, it spirals completely out of control.

Self-care allows you to reduce the stress you are experiencing and to actually calm down enough to ensure that you can still function in a productive manner, regardless of your ADHD. Quite often this is achieved through the most basic forms of self-care, such as having frequent and nourishing meals.

Proper self-care can also have a positive impact on your self-esteem and self-confidence. This will be done through motivating yourself, celebrating your achievements, and engaging in positive affirmations. All these will have an impact on your opinion of yourself and can help to greatly improve this. This is extremely beneficial to people with ADHD, as we often tend to suffer from low self-esteem due to the difficulties that we face with normal functions in life.

We also tend to be more prone to becoming overwhelmed and burnt out. This is because part of losing focus on the task at hand is overthinking. When you add the elevated levels of stress we tend to endure then this is a real challenge that people with ADHD tend to face. When we engage in self-care, we allow ourselves to rest and recharge, and to better regulate our energy levels and mental state. Self-care can also help us to prioritize our needs which will help to decrease our stress and exhaustion levels. Additionally, self-care also helps us to implement healthy boundaries.

Self-care is of the utmost importance for those of us with ADHD as it helps us to manage our symptoms. I want you to remember that there is no shame in looking after yourself at times. We are often told to look after those around us before we look after ourselves. While being selfless is a good thing, you won't have the energy to be selfless if you don't look after yourself first.

Exercise

In this exercise we'll be exercising both a form of self-care, as well as tracking our goals. Part of both of these is to celebrate our achievements and to make note of them. So, this exercise will need you to complete it on the go. As you establish a routine, and work towards your goals you can complete this exercise. Of course, I will show you an example first, and then supply you with an empty template.

Example

Goal: Exercising daily.	Date: 01/07/2023
Previous Achievements:	
Date	**Achievement**
01/01/2023	First day of exercises completed.
01/03/2023	Three consecutive days completed
01/04/2023	Muscles are no longer sore.

New Achievements:

Date	Achievement
01/07/2023	One week of consecutive daily exercise completed
01/07/2023	Managed to jog around the block without becoming winded for the first time.
01/07/2023	Woke up before my alarm for the first time.

Your Turn

Goal:	Date: __/__/____
Previous Achievements:	
Date	**Achievement**
New Achievements:	
Date	**Achievement**

Implementing Healthy Habits

CHAPTER 5

Overcoming Obstacles and Staying Motivated

Obstacles don't have to stop you. If you run into a wall, don't turn around and give up. Figure out how to climb it, go through it, or work around it.

–Michael Jordan

Of course, no habits can be formed or changed without a learning opportunity along the way. There are no better learning opportunities than failing. A failure gives you a front-row seat to see what goes wrong, which also means that you have the best perspective to learn what not to do. In this chapter, we will be looking at what steps you can take to overcome the obstacles that will find you while ensuring that you remain motivated along the way.

Common Obstacles That Can Derail Habit-Building Efforts

When you are in the process of building new habits, encountering obstacles is guaranteed. This is a non-negotiable aspect of any part of life. The key to successfully dealing with obstacles is to recognize when you come face-to-face with an obstacle and develop effective strategies to deal with these obstacles.

First, let's look into the possible challenges you might face. The first obstacle we'll be focusing on is the lack of consistency. As we've already established it is extremely difficult for someone with ADHD to remain consistent in their behavior. This can be due to your ADHD symptoms, or because of outside influences. You could easily get bored with the same monotone routine that you are following daily. This is why we need to allow a measure of flexibility in our routines, while also taking steps to ensure it remains interesting to us.

However, just as easily as our own minds can get in our way, the outside world can come in like a wrecking ball and just leave havoc in its way. I've mentioned this earlier as well, an unexpected traffic jam, a family emergency, or any type of disruption to your routine can throw all your progress out of the window. The key to dealing with this is to ensure that you are prepared for it. Have a backup routine planned and create alternative times for the tasks that need to be completed. Plan for failure so that when it occurs you can take it in stride instead of having to break your stride.

The next challenge in forming habits is another one we are already familiar with, but that deserves to be repeated. We can easily feel overwhelmed by our goals. The interesting part is that it might not be your goal specifically that overwhelms you. For example, while researching this book I obviously searched a lot of ADHD content. As we all know by now, the cookies we constantly agree to when accessing websites are used to ensure that the advertisements and content that we see on the internet are catered to our individual interests. So, when after spending a whole day researching I rewarded myself with an hour of doom scrolling, I found my social media filled with content that relates to ADHD. While normally I would find this interesting and probably go down a rabbit hole with this, it was simply too close to my goal of finishing this book.

This meant that instead of allowing my mind to take a break, I started to feel overwhelmed and had to find other avenues of releasing dopamine and taking a break. This further shows that challenges can arise when we least expect it. Our goals can start to feel overwhelmed by small influences that are only loosely related to the goals. To combat this obstacle, we must ensure that we set our goals in small, achievable increments while working toward larger goals. While at the same time taking steps to ensure that normal life does not become overwhelming for our goals.

Our difficulties with our executive functions lead us to the next obstacle. As I've just mentioned, it is imperative that we plan and prepare not just for how we will change our habits, but also for what we can do if our routines and habits are interrupted. To prepare and plan better for habits and failures we can take steps such as preparing our ingredients for our meals in advance. Plan out your meals for the entire week and take one day in a week to prepare all the ingredients. Label them and put them aside so that when you want to cook your meal, all you need to do is remove the ingredients from their containers and add them to your meal. That way your goal of eating healthier has less chance of being overwhelming, and if you face a delay in your routine and you need to eat later than usual, you are less likely to get fast food in order to save time. The same idea can be adapted to any of your habits and goals. Pre-plan your outfits for the week and hang them up together, pack your gym bag the day before, and prepare your workspace before leaving for the day, so that when you get to work the next morning you can just jump in.

You will need to use trial and error to determine what preparations and planning make your life easier, and which ones make you feel overwhelmed. It is entirely possible that too much planning and preparation can have a negative influence on you. If you focus too much on the planning and preparation this becomes a task for you that can easily snowball into a huge pile of anxiety.

These obstacles can be a lot harder to overcome if you find yourself facing them alone. When you don't have someone that you can share your pain and concerns with, you tend to internalize these emotions. This leads to poor mental health and a variety of conditions such as anxiety and depression. We as people with ADHD have a greater difficulty in regulating our emotions, which is why it is important that you do not internalize your feelings and emotions. Instead, finding some sort of support system can help you to not only deal with setbacks better but also help calm you down when you start to feel overwhelmed or that your goals might be unachievable.

The other perk that a support system offers you, is that you now also have someone to hold you accountable. This doesn't mean your support buddy should be reprimanding you or tracking your progress for you. It could be something as simple as telling them that you want to achieve a certain goal in a certain timeframe. By just telling this information to someone you are already creating a measure of accountability that can be self-enforced. Be sure that you communicate the level of accountability you require to your support system. We all deal with life in different ways, so your level of accountability needs will almost certainly be different from mine.

Because we also need to ensure that we receive as much dopamine as possible from our actions to ensure that we enjoy completing them, the lack of immediate rewards could also be an obstacle for us. While this is not a mechanism that works with everyone, most people with ADHD need some sort of immediate reward to function as positive reinforcement. When we are rewarded immediately our brain associates the resulting dopamine with the action that we just completed which makes this action feel more fulfilling. The reward you give yourself will also be based on what works for you as an individual. For some people, a small treat like a chocolate after a finished task will be enough, while for others a 15-minute social media break might be more fitting, or perhaps a 30-minute reading time. Your reward is completely based on what you as a person enjoy.

Another form of rewarding yourself is to celebrate each milestone and achievement. This is once again based on your personal needs and interests as an individual. Some people enjoy posting their achievements on social media, others enjoy showing them off to their friends in person. While another person might enjoy commemorating the special occasion by indulging themselves a bit. Remember that your reward is based on what you as an individual require. Whether it is buying yourself a new outfit because it fits better or going to see a movie in the cinema because you've managed to complete all your work on time for the past month, it is completely up to you to decide.

During this section, so far, we've alluded a lot to the impact that your emotions and stress can have on your journey into forming new habits. This is due to the fact that emotions and stress both can be an obstacle in their own right. As we've already covered before, when we become stressed, anxious, or depressed, our ADHD symptoms tend to flare up. This is caused by the fact that emotional triggers prohibit our bodies from creating more dopamine. As we already know our body lacks dopamine and other "happy chemicals" which means that when our bodies create even less of these chemicals we end up with more severe symptoms. These symptoms will mean that we have more difficulty maintaining our focus and concentrating on our tasks. To combat this, you need to ensure that you keep your emotional welfare in mind at all times. Self-care is an amazing way to look after your mental and emotional health. Aside from that you also need to identify what your emotional needs are, while ensuring that you meet them and reduce stress as much as possible. Another key aspect in managing your emotional triggers is to ensure that you have healthy coping mechanisms and you get rid of any negative and unhealthy coping mechanisms. Be warned, these unhealthy coping mechanisms often lead right back to negative and unhealthy habits and behaviors.

All these obstacles and changes in your life mean that you need to be extremely adaptable. Life in general needs you to be extremely adaptable but when you are attempting to make meaningful changes to your life you need to be even more adaptable. This is why backup plans are so important. They allow us to adapt to almost anything. Let's say for example that your local gym accidentally floods. This will keep the gym out of commission for quite a while and leave you with a problem.

What is your backup plan in a situation like this? The unpredictability of life means that you need to be able to adapt to any situation, whether likely to happen or not. You will also need to be able to adapt your life and your routine to others. You might enjoy preparing your workspace a day in advance, but your boss might want you to keep your workspace completely cleared when you are done for the day. Then again you will need to come up with an entirely new plan.

The final obstacle we will cover in your path to creating new habits is you. This might be the biggest obstacle that will ever stand in your way. Your inner saboteur might whisper little negative remarks to you that can cause you to doubt yourself. These might be remarks telling you that you will never reach your goals, or that you will never be able to implement positive change and will never be able to stick with these changes. In a later section, we will look into positive affirmations as these are the most effective way to combat that negative voice inside your head. However, that should not be the only measure you take against your inner saboteur. You also need to be compassionate towards yourself and learn to recognize your own strengths and successes. This is usually made easier by surrounding yourself with a positive environment. Remove anyone from your life that tries to break you down or who does not actively support you and celebrate your success. The more you cultivate a positive environment around you, the more you will create a positive environment within yourself.

When building habits, you will inevitably fail. This is not something you should fear, however. Instead, you should embrace this. By embracing your failures, you make them a part of your journey instead of a danger to your progress. The only way to do this is to plan for it and be well-prepared. By arming yourself with persistence and resilience you will succeed. I also want to remind you not to expect immediate results. We all grow and change at different speeds. This means that you should not try to compare yourself to others. Just because you know of someone that managed to make changes very quickly, it does not mean that you are failing if you cannot do the same.

Strategies for Overcoming Procrastination, Perfectionism, and Other Challenges

As I've mentioned we need to strategize for our challenges. While in the previous section, I mentioned some major obstacles we might face and gave some advice to overcome these challenges, they are not the only challenges that we might face. Our ADHD can often cause us to be perfectionists and unwilling to accept any of our work unless it is of an unrealistic quality that we desire.

When we cannot achieve this level of quality we tend to start feeling anxious and overwhelmed about our work, usually, the best way for us to then cope with this is by procrastinating so that we don't focus on our work. The way our brains work allows us to very quickly forget something if we do not constantly see or think about it. So, procrastination allows a release from life and its stress.

Of course, we don't always need stress or our perfectionism to lure us into procrastination. Procrastination on its own is always a danger to someone with ADHD. We also have a wide variety of other challenges that we need to prepare for, so let's look into a few strategies that we can implement in our life to help improve the quality of our life and eliminate obstacles before we encounter them.

The first strategy to look into is to make sure that you have clear deadlines for your goals. Make sure that your deadlines are realistic and flexible when needed. This will give you a sense of accountability and make it easier to prioritize what actions are more urgent than others.

Of course, as we know by now it can be extremely detrimental to only focus on the end goal. I've already suggested that you break your goals down into much smaller, more achievable steps. So, make sure that you give these steps a timeline as well. This doesn't have to be a strict deadline but can be more of a guideline such as giving yourself ten minutes in the morning to ready your workspace or ensuring that you pack the dishwasher within fifteen minutes after you finished eating. In this way, you give yourself a flexible deadline in small steps which will make it easier to achieve your end goal.

When you focus on finishing this one small step within a certain time period, you'll be able to ensure that you complete your larger goal in a timely manner. If you decide that your larger goal is to finish all your dishes by 10 p.m. every night. You can break up your smaller tasks and allot yourself the time that you would need for each step to ensure that you do accomplish your goal by 10 p.m.

Of course, this is not the only time management technique that is available to you. I would suggest looking into the different techniques that have proven to work for others and experimenting to find out which of these work the best for you.

One such technique that often shows extremely positive results is called the Pomodoro technique. This technique requires you to focus on your work for 25 minutes, which is then followed by a five-minute break. After the fourth consecutive work interval, referred to as a Pomodoro, a longer break of 15 to 30 minutes can be taken. This technique could always be adapted to what works better for you. For example, I tend to work for an hour straight. During this hour my phone is often turned off and left out of reach to ensure that I do not act on the impulse of simply picking up my phone and procrastinating. After an hour of constant work, I tend to reward myself with a 15-minute break during which time I sit outside and away from work. To help me focus during my hour of work I also remove all clocks from my surroundings so I cannot watch the time, and I play soft classical music with no lyrics in the background.

The reason I choose to use music with no lyrics is that I find it easy to start focusing on the words of a song, which then leads my mind astray and removes my focus from the work at hand. While this works quite well for me, you might be a bit different and use music with lyrics, or even a radio station. Remember, different things work for different people. It's also important to note that often when we are working in complete silence, it allows our brains to start creating background noise for us due to our ADHD causing a shift in our focus. When there is nothing that we can focus on, our mind creates something. This often means that our mind can be more interesting than some actual background noise.

Another technique that has proven quite effective is called time blocking. When we talk about time blocking you allocate a certain time period to a single task. For example, from 9:00 a.m. until 9:15 a.m. your time is blocked out and allocated to reading and answering emails. During that time, you do absolutely nothing other than reading your mails and answering them. If someone brings you other work that has to be done during that time the work is put aside. This technique requires more than just self-control, but also communication and the ability to enforce boundaries. You should be able to communicate to others that you are blocking out this time for certain tasks, and even be able to communicate to people if they are interfering with the task allotted to this time.

If you find yourself more often distracted by your phone, you can try switching your phone off and leaving it in a different room. However, in these modern times, we have become so used to constantly being connected to each other. This often means that leaving our phones in a different room can cause severe anxiety in case someone needs to reach us in the event of an emergency. In cases like these, you could also download a variety of apps and software that locks you out of using certain websites and apps like Facebook and Instagram. These apps and software can all be installed on both your phone and computer and still allows you to receive phone calls and access messaging apps when there is an emergency.

While these techniques are quite effective at helping to stop you from procrastinating or losing your focus, they can also help you in regard to your perfectionism. Before we continue I want to clarify what the problem with perfectionism is. After all, making sure your work is absolutely perfect sounds like it's supposed to be a good thing. The problem with this, however, is that perfectionism can be extremely time-consuming to start off with. We tend to want to start a project completely from scratch if we deem it not to be up to our standards. This can often lead to the project taking much longer than it needs to be.

There is another pitfall connected to perfectionism. This is called analysis paralysis. People with ADHD are more prone to suffering from analysis paralysis since it is caused by anxiety which we already know we are more prone to suffering from. When we suffer from analysis paralysis we find it impossible to make even the smallest decisions. This is because we are torn between the feelings of being completely unhappy about our work so far, but not being sure how to improve it, and being unhappy with our own attempts at improvement. This is an impossible situation to be in. It is an even more difficult situation to get yourself out of because once you are in it, it is almost impossible to get rid of the feelings that caused the situation to form in the first place.

The key to getting ahead of the game. Accept that you might not reach your preferred quality level of perfection before you even start your project. Accept that it is better to finish your project than it is to never finish it because you are always attempting to improve upon it. This does not mean that you will or should do a poor job, instead, it means that you should accept when something is not entirely perfect. Once you have finished your project, if there is still more time left before your deadline you can use that time to further improve on the quality of your work. You will find that your innate need for perfectionism will most often mean that your work exceeds expectations before you even start making improvements.

I want to reiterate self-compassion at this time. We've dealt with procrastination and perfectionism now. Both of these allude to the fact that you might not be completely happy with your own work. This is often rooted deep within your own self-doubt and poor self-esteem. Although I have mentioned self-compassion and self-care quite a bit by now, I want you to remember that

ADHD is a mental health condition. That means it will affect your mental health greatly which is why I continuously reiterate the importance of proper mental health care and being compassionate and understanding when it comes to yourself. Your mindset and your mental health require more attention and positive support than a neurotypical person does.

This level of mental health care is quite difficult to achieve alone. This is also why I have been so adamant about creating a supportive environment that includes people who actively assist you in keeping you accountable and motivating you. I understand that at times our ADHD could make us socially awkward and prefer ourselves to be loners. There is also the addition of object permanence which relates to people as well. Those of us with ADHD tend to "forget" our relationship with friends and family members if we don't interact with them on a frequent basis.

An effective solution to this problem is often to include our support partner in our activities. For example, if your goals are in relation to your career then it might be beneficial to make friends with a coworker. You will regularly see this person, in the environment in which you are attempting to make changes, and they will understand your goals as well. You also don't need to make this person your best friend. I don't want you to feel pressured into a situation that you might not be comfortable with at all. However, a simple conversation with this person on a regular basis might help. You can also decide to be completely honest with this person and ask them if they would be willing to be your accountability partner and offer to do the same for them.

Alternatively, you can also find people with similar goals online. I have a group of other people that are also writing their own books. We even communicate with each other on an instant messaging app where we update each other on the progress of our books, and at times even write together. When we do this we track our progress, look at how many words we each type for the day, and we motivate each other to write even more. In this manner, we don't have to communicate with each other when we don't want to, and we don't have to let each other into our personal lives at all. This is a very easy way to find accountability partners without an imposition on our personal lives.

This also helps to create a supportive environment as we can also have discussions with each other about difficulties we face while working towards our goal. This is made easier since we all share similar goals. I also understand that this type of supportive environment might not work for everyone. That is why it is important for you to take a leap of faith and try out different ways of creating a supportive environment. You can find mobile phone apps to do this, or just try to change your physical environment to be more supportive.

While not an extensive list here are a few tips for creating a supportive environment for yourself;

- Take steps against your critics. Make sure to limit contact with people that break you down and spend more time with those that build you up.

- Recognize what makes you doubt yourself and take steps to remove these triggers from your life. As I've mentioned to you before, these triggers might not be directly connected or related to your stressors but could be loosely connected to your goals.

- Be sure you remind yourself why you are pursuing your goals. We'll look more into this point in a moment when we deal with affirmations.

- Be proactive with the steps you take. If you have identified self-doubt as one of the main obstacles in your journey, don't wait until you doubt yourself to motivate yourself. Make sure to battle your obstacles before they impede your progress.

- Make sure the people in your life share your goals and values. When people have like-minded perspectives in life they will be an asset on your journey.

Another effective strategy to use to overcome obstacles is something that might sound absolutely ridiculous to you. The key here is to use visualization. When you can visualize yourself succeeding you are telling yourself that it is a possibility. This helps you to reduce feelings of stress and anxiety and help you feel less overwhelmed. The problem with visualization is that most people often do not believe that visualization is an effective technique. Visualization is more than just imagining that you have succeeded or daydreaming about having a perfect life. When you are visualizing your success, you need to visualize succeeding in every step along the way.

While I've already covered using rewards to trick your brain into releasing the happy chemicals it so sorely needs as a way to ensure success, you can also use this in a proactive way to prepare for, and combat obstacles before they arise. If you give yourself incentives you are able to motivate yourself before you even start your task. The way this is done is by deciding what your reward will be beforehand and setting strict requirements for yourself to be eligible for that reward.

This will look something along the lines of saying that you will be allowed a piece of your favorite guilty pleasure dessert if you finish your dishes by 9 p.m. each day for a week. If you fail at doing this, simply restart counting the days instead of punishing yourself for failing. This is a fine line between knowing when you are giving yourself an incentive and when you are withholding something from yourself as a punishment.

Finally, I want to remind you that not only do you not need to go through this alone, but you can also get professional help if you need it. Never underestimate the help that a fully trained mental health practitioner can offer you. There is unfortunately a stigma attached to mental health. Many people believe that if you see a mental health practitioner on a regular basis that there must be something wrong with you. This, of course, is not true. Mental health practitioners can be excellent resources in proactively combatting possible obstacles in your way and preparing for any challenges you might face.

At the same time, there is also a world of resources available to you. By buying and reading this book you have actually already taken the first step into collecting resources and teaching yourself more about ADHD and how to deal with it. The internet has also become a great resource and social media apps are being used by not only healthcare professionals but also experts in the field to spread awareness and information regarding conditions such as ADHD, Autism, Bipolar Personality Disorder, and so many other conditions. I do however invite you to properly research and validate any information you may find online. While there are many people attempting to do good in the world and break the stigma around mental health, there are unfortunately still people around that spread misinformation. This is however not always done on purpose and this makes misinformation even more difficult to spot.

Affirmations

I've decided to give affirmations special attention in their own section. This is because affirmations can be extremely helpful in motivating you, building up your self-esteem, creating a positive and supportive environment, and even helping to look after your mental health.

A positive affirmation is a mantra or a phrase that is meant to be repeated in order to build up your focus, confidence, and even motivation. You can create your own affirmation phrases or find some basic ones on the internet and choose the ones that align with what you are trying to achieve.

When you have chosen your affirmations, you have a few options on how you can repeat them to yourself. The most popular way is to print them out or to write them down on sticky notes and paste them in places where you will regularly see them. This can be on your bathroom mirror, next to your bed, somewhere in your car, on your desk at work, inside your gym bag, or anywhere that you know you will be every day. You can also set daily reminders on your phone with the affirmation as your title for the reminders. In this way, you will receive the message via your phone at a certain time each day and need to dismiss the reminder, which gives you a chance to read the affirmation. You can also save the affirmations in the Notes app on your phone and computer and read the affirmations when you feel the need to.

Finally, I suggest when you read your affirmations that you read them aloud and repeat them at least three times. Of course, this is only a suggestion and you should find what works for you and follow that.

To help you get started with affirmations here are a few that you can use:

- I have ADHD, now watch me be awesome!

- I have the ability to do anything I put my mind to.

- I believe in myself. I have faith in myself.

- I trust my own abilities.

- Everything I do is good enough.

- I can choose to let negativity go.

- I can succeed on my own. Just imagine what I can do with some help.

- My way may be different, but that doesn't mean it's not the right way.

- I have all the time in the world to succeed.

You might be wondering if something as simple as repeating a positive message to yourself truly works. To answer this, I have a question in return, have you ever heard the phrase "They lie so much that they start to believe themselves?" That is basically what you will be doing. When you constantly hear the same positive phrase repeated you will actually start to believe it, to the point where it will actually start to change your mindset completely. Yes, there have been studies done on the power and effectiveness of positive affirmations in which it was proven to be effective.

Finally, your affirmations can also be as specific as you want them to be. While the affirmations I've given you so far are just general affirmations, you can create your own affirmations that are specific to you and your goal. Think of something along the lines of "I will lose twenty pounds before summer."

Overcoming challenges like perfectionism or procrastination is not easy. This is because these challenges are caused by your own mind and aspects of your personality. This means that changing it will require constant effort and quite a lot of your time. It will not be an easy task so please be patient and give yourself some grace. You have all the tools needed to succeed. In fact, you have always had it within you to succeed. By using the right strategies and phishing you can overcome any obstacle in your way, and yes this includes procrastination, perfectionism, and whatever other difficulties are thrown in your path.

Tips for Staying Motivated and Maintaining Progress Over Time

One of the main requirements for success is motivation. We need to ensure that you remain motivated to follow your goals at all times. While up until now we've been looking at this fact in general, it is now time to focus on your motivation.

Before we look at the new tips I want to offer you, let's just take a moment to recap what we already know. The goals that you set for yourself need to mean something to you. As noble as it might be to pursue goals that are important to others for whatever reason, you will not be able to find the motivation to succeed in these goals if they are not close to your heart as well.

Once you've chosen the correct goals they need to be broken into smaller, more easily achievable milestones. Think of your goals as a very long road trip. If you only care about the end destination then it will take you a very long time before you get there. If, however, you find a few destinations and attractions along the way to visit, then your road trip becomes infinitely more entertaining and fulfilling.

Just like most people in the modern world will use social media to check in where they stop and take a picture of the attraction they stopped there to see, you should also keep a record of your journey towards achieving your goals. This allows you to see how far you have come, what you have achieved, and how much you've overcome.

This is all information that we've covered before so I won't go into more detail regarding this, instead let's look forward to other tips that can help you stay motivated.

The first of the new tips is to find intrinsic motivation. This is when you find enjoyment and fulfillment in an activity. The intrinsic motivation should be derived from the habits you are trying to form. I realize that this sounds vague and impossible.

So, let me explain better with an example; when you are busy cleaning the dishes, take some time to enjoy how clean your home feels. Enjoy the extra space and lavish in the feelings of relaxation and pride that overcomes you. You will need to make a conscious effort to find enjoyment and allow your body to release happy chemicals for you. By finding enjoyment in your new habits you will want to engage in these habits which will in turn help you remain motivated.

Earlier we looked into visualization as a way to overcome obstacles, but visualization techniques can also be used to motivate you. While you can ensure your success by visualizing yourself accomplishing the tasks, you visualize yourself enjoying these tasks and completing them with ease. When you believe that these tasks will be fun and easy to complete, you will be motivated enough to do so.

While I have been encouraging you to look to the future and to your success the entire time, I also want you to remember why you are doing all of this. Why are you attempting to make these changes? If, for example, your goal was to improve your eating habits, to in turn lose weight, you risk the possibility of forgetting why you changed your habits when you've reached your goal weight. To ensure that you do not forget why, you will need to remind yourself of the reason on a regular basis. Doing this will help to keep you motivated.

Your motivation will falter at times. This is one of the most dangerous obstacles that you will face. In fact, you will eventually fail due to a lack of motivation. This is a normal part of your journey, a part that we will all experience at some point. I have experienced it myself, and I have no doubt that my motivation will falter in the future again. But through perseverance and picking ourselves up, and trying again, we will succeed.

Exercise

This is the final exercise before we put it all together. In this exercise, we'll be looking at the obstacles we believe we will be facing, and we will be making contingency plans that we can fall back on instead.

Example

Goal	I want to workout every day after work.
Obstacle	The gym I am a member of might close unexpectedly.
Affirmation	I control my body, and I can achieve the goals I have for it.

Contingency Plan

If the gym closes down unexpectedly then I will be following a home workout routine instead. I have a one-week cardio-intensive program that can keep me busy in the interim. If the gym remains closed longer than a week I will adjust this plan to include basic strength training as well.

New Schedule

Monday

16:30	Leave work and go home.
16:45	Arrive home and change clothes.
17:00	Do stretches and warm-up exercises for five minutes.
17:05	Run 5 miles.
18:00	Do 3 sets of burpees
18:10	Do 3 sets of mountain climbers.

Your Turn

The template below is left extremely blank in order to allow you to adjust it to any goal that you may have. The above example should guide you in how to adapt it to your needs.

Goal	
Obstacle	
Affirmation	
Contingency Plan	
New Schedule	

Overcoming Obstacles and Staying Motivated

___:___	
___:___	
___:___	
___:___	
___:___	
___:___	

CHAPTER 6

Putting It All Together

The chapters until this point have all been like pieces of a puzzle. Now we need to put these puzzle pieces together so we can find our goals. It won't be as easy as just putting all the exercises in a list, however. You will need to look at each section individually and as a whole.

Strategies for Adapting the Plan to Your Individual Needs and Lifestyle

I hope that thus far I've made it clear enough that while all of us with ADHD face similar challenges, symptoms, and problems, these will all each present themselves differently to each individual; which also means that each individual will need to deal with them differently. So, while the plans, exercises and advice in this workbook are all excellent for people with ADHD, there is only so much use that can be gathered from this book if you are unable to adapt it to your individual needs.

To start identifying your personal needs, you need to get to know yourself. Figure out what your strengths are, what your weaknesses are, what you like, and what you don't like. You need to understand your own personality and emotions. It might be difficult to truly understand who and what you are, especially since we are conditioned by society to believe we should be a certain way.

You will find that you often become confused by what you believe you should be, and who you truly are. In some instances, you might be able to find yourself easily, and in other instances, it will take time and a lot of self-reflection to discover when something is not working for you. Keep an open mind and listen to both your mind and body to learn your own rhythm.

When you have discovered your true self, you need to identify the outside influences that are unique to you. For example, while one person may have very flexible working hours, you might be constrained to certain working hours. You may work 12-hour shifts, while someone else works only 8-hour shifts. When you have a family or even roommates to also look after your time constraints may differ as well. You might need to be home at a certain time or need to have dinner ready at a certain time. These are constraints and commitments that you need to identify. You will need to look at each commitment and realize what times and activities are already set in stone, and which you can move around and adjust to make your schedule and routine work better for you.

You will also need to identify how much energy your existing commitments will require. I often feel like I have only a certain amount of social interactions in me, almost like a social battery that gets drained after a while. Eventually, you learn to understand your own social battery, and you understand how much of yourself you can give others. For example, I know that I can spend around four hours in the company of someone that does not require hard work to communicate with before I become restless and overstimulated. However, when it comes to someone that enjoys complaining or creating high-stress environments, I can at best hold out an hour before I start to feel overwhelmed by their presence.

So, what does this mean? When planning my day, I know how much time I can allocate to social interactions based on the people I will be interacting with. When I have family commitments I can allocate about two hours towards social interactions, when I'm going out with friends I can allocate up to six hours. If I have a meeting planned for the day with someone I don't know, then I try to plan no other social interactions for that day in order to make sure I don't overextend my social battery. You will need to identify your social capabilities and ensure that you adapt your routines and habits to your needs.

Social interactions are one of many factors in life that we are unable to control. Aside from that, remember that we've already established our ADHD makes it easier for us to become bored with a strict schedule. This is why when you are initially starting a new routine, it is recommended that you create more than one schedule for your new routine. You can also try to set deadlines instead of time schedules. So instead of saying that you should wake up every morning at 7 a.m., you set a deadline that you should be awake by 8 a.m. This allows you to wake up at whatever time is convenient for you while keeping your schedule flexible and interesting.

While you are adjusting your day and the time available to suit your needs, you should also adapt your environment to work with you. This can be something simple like changing the layout of your kitchen, or like I suggested earlier, hanging your clothes in ready-to-wear outfits in your cupboard so that you can just grab and go. This is also applicable to your workspace to ensure there are as little distractions as possible.

Another strategy to adapt these plans to your individual personality is to incorporate your interests into your habits and routines. Let's say for example that you really like strawberries and your goal is to create healthier eating habits; you can try to find recipes that include strawberries so that you have an easier time adapting to this new habit. If you like dancing and want to become more active and fit, try signing up for a dance class as part of your exercise routine. There are many ways to incorporate your own interests into your habits, but you might need to get creative if you want to keep it interesting enough for your ADHD to not be too much of an obstacle.

While you are trying to find the perfect plan to suit your needs you will need to experiment with different techniques and adaptations. You might think that playing music while you are working will help you to focus since music is one of your interests. But when you try and listen to your favorite band while working you might find yourself even more distracted. This means that you will need to experiment with different genres, and even with not playing music. When you find something that seems like it works you will need to try it for a while and monitor yourself closely to see if this will work in the long run or not. While doing this you need to adjust your habits and routines as you go, otherwise you risk stagnating and falling back into old habits.

While I have all the faith in the world in the tools I've provided in this book, I also want to invite you to make full use of any and all technology at your disposal. This technology can be in the form of an app. You'll find that there are many apps available on smartphones that also help you to create a schedule, set reminders, and even remain focused on your preferred tasks. The main problem with these apps is that they usually require a monthly subscription to use effectively.

Finally, another effective strategy to ensure that you are adapting these routines to you as an individual is to get feedback on whether there is any progress towards your goals. I've already suggested to you that you should get a support system going. Your support system does not only have to motivate you but can also help you to keep track and ensure that your routine is working. Those around you can tell you whether they can see any of the changes you are implementing, and even help you to keep an eye out for signs of regression and failure.

What we are trying to do with this workbook is to give you access to personalized tools that will work for you and help you to better function in your day-to-day life, as well as improve the quality of your life, despite your ADHD diagnosis. This means that you will need to constantly evaluate, adapt, and make the changes you require. The tips I just shared with you should help you to personalize these tools, but again, you might need to take a different approach or try new techniques that I haven't shared here. Luckily, I have faith that you will be able to do so. Remember, asking for help is always an option as well.

Full Exercise

Now that you have all the tools required at your disposal and know how to personalize them all to your needs, doing so and getting started should not be difficult. In this section, you will do a combination of all the exercises that we've done so far. While I do encourage you to do each exercise on your own, then fill in the full exercise, the choice remains yours. This final exercise will also not include all of the sections that previous exercises involve. This exercise is meant to be an overall schedule that can be used once you have worked through the other exercises.

What is your goal?	
Break your goal into tasks	1.
	2.
	3.
	4.
	5.
	6.
	7.
	8.
	9.
	10.

Break your tasks into smaller steps.	
Schedule	
Morning	
__:__	
__:__	

__:__	
__:__	
__:__	

Work Time

__:__	
__:__	
__:__	
__:__	
__:__	
__:__	
__:__	
__:__	

__:__	
__:__	
Evening	
__:__	
__:__	
__:__	
__:__	
__:__	
__:__	
__:__	
__:__	
__:__	

Plan B	
Obstacle	
Affirmation	
Contingency Plan	
New Schedule	
__:__	
__:__	
__:__	

___:___	
___:___	
___:___	

Conclusion

Living with ADHD is not always easy. At the same time, it does not need to be difficult. None of us asked to be different or to be born with ADHD. Unfortunately, this is a part of life.

While we cannot definitively pinpoint the cause of ADHD yet, we have been able to make great progress in understanding ADHD. While in the past people with ADHD have most often been misdiagnosed as just being lazy, or even less intelligent than others, we now understand that this is not truly the case.

While our understanding has begun to increase this has not truly broken the stigma attached to ADHD or helped to educate the general population. In fact, there are still plenty of people that have been diagnosed with ADHD that also lack proper education on what this means. This is in part due to the fact that we are seeing many more adults being positively diagnosed since they were misdiagnosed during childhood.

In addition to this, there is also still a major stigma attached to mental health in general. A great deal of society still believes that if anyone requires any type of mental health assistance it means that there is something extremely wrong with them and that they are most probably dangerous as well. This belief is often reinforced when words such as disorder are used. Disorder itself has a negative connotation as it means the opposite of order and stability.

When you are not seen as being potentially violent, it is believed that you are unstable and completely unable to regulate your own emotions. Take a moment and think about this. Does this sound like you? Of course, it does not. While we might find it more difficult to regulate our own emotions, we don't normally lose all control over ourselves or pose a danger to society in any way. We are most definitely also not less intelligent than the average person.

All ADHD means is that our mind functions in a different way and that we need a little more positivity in our lives than other people do. We need to make sure that our brains receive the chemicals that it has difficulty making on their own. By doing this we ensure that we function in a more neurotypical manner. Although, I do not want to make you believe that you should act completely neurotypical.

I like seeing ADHD as a type of superpower. ADHD is almost the definition of a jack of all trades. This is because the mixture of hyper fixations and difficulty focusing allows us to pursue many skills and hobbies, often at the same time.

We tend to also be able to move on from emotional pain and distress a lot faster than neurotypical people because our brain allows us to forget something faster when it is no longer prevalent in our daily lives.

Of course, all these superpowers come with their own Achilles Heel. The difficulties in focusing can impact our productivity. The hyper fixations can cause time blindness, and "out of sight, out of mind" can apply to our loved ones, work, and even to our health as we often forget to eat and exercise on a regular basis.

These are all the reasons why we need to implement routines and healthy habits. These will allow us to subdue the negative side effects of ADHD while capitalizing on the positive side effects. In short, we will make our mental health work for us. Doing this, however, can be extremely difficult and we need to take certain steps to ensure that we maintain our progress in the long run.

While we know that we will falter at times, we still do whatever we can to ensure that we do not relapse and fall back into our old habits. This is not an easy feat to accomplish. It will require constant effort from your side, and even then, it may not always be enough.

To do this you need to remain committed to your goals and regularly remind yourself of why you are engaging in these habits. This is why the second chapter and its exercise are so important. This allows you to write down what your goals are and why you are pursuing these goals. When you fail or falter you can take out the exercise you completed to help you get back on track.

In the fourth chapter, we have an exercise that allows you to track your progress. This is important because it helps you to keep an eye on your achievements. I also want to encourage you to start a diary or journal, as this allows you more freedom to share your thoughts and emotions. You can also add picture evidence of your progress when it's possible. Remember that when you can look back on your journey and see what you have accomplished, it allows you to feel good about your journey. This not only helps to motivate you for your future progress, but it can also help your mind to release the happy chemicals needed to improve your executive functions.

Tracking your progress like this also has another benefit. It gives you the opportunity to celebrate your achievements. Whenever you reach a specific milestone or add another goal to the exercise sheet in chapter four, I want you to print out the entire list and paste it somewhere near your daily affirmations where you will see it regularly. This allows you to double your daily motivation.

You will also be able to use these exercises to keep yourself accountable. You will be able to see when you have to start your goals over again, and you will see which goals you are struggling with. If you have a friend or support system going through these exercises with you, the two of you can use these exercises to hold each other accountable as well.

You will also need to constantly review your progress and reflect on whether or not you are moving closer to your success or not. Additionally, you will need to plan for setbacks as well. This is where the exercise in the fifth chapter comes into play. This exercise will allow you to take any failures and obstacles in stride and that you never have to worry about not being able to get up. Failing to plan, is planning to fail, and this exercise will ensure that you do not fail to plan at all.

You can implement these contingency plans at the drop of a hat. Oftentimes you will need to do so. Remember to remain vigilant for warning signs that you might be losing your motivation, or that you are no longer making any progress. When you see these signs, you might need to switch to your plan B immediately, or even create a new plan altogether.

This is what is called being flexible, and I hope that you have seen that it is possible to plan your flexibility. Have your adjustments ready and know when you need to be more strict, or even less strict with yourself. I also want you to remember that you are continuously changing as a person, and so are your needs. This will mean that you will not only need to evaluate your techniques on a continuous basis but also your goals. Ensure that they remain important to you. At the same time, you need to keep an eye on when your mental health and even interests change, as this can affect your ADHD symptoms, which in turn affects what techniques are effective for you.

Part of doing this is also staying up to date with the newest and latest information on ADHD. By continuously learning about your condition, you will allow yourself to learn new strategies and techniques that may not even exist yet.

Finally, you need to look after yourself at all times. This will be in the form of both self-care and self-compassion. Additionally, remaining connected to your support system will also assist in this. This entire book is about helping you to improve and to do that, there needs to be a you that wants to improve.

My hope is that this book helps all those with ADHD to not only better understand themselves but to also show the world that ADHD is not something to ridicule or be ashamed of. Just as some people have different eye colors, so do some people have brains that function slightly differently.

We are still normal, we are still humans, we are just slightly more interesting.

References

10 Quotes on Overcoming Obstacles That Will Motivate You. (2021, July 15). Teamphoria. https://www.teamphoria.com/10-quotes-on-overcoming-obstacles-that-will-motivate-you/

75 Quotes About Achieving Goals To Inspire and Motivate You. (n.d.). Indeed Career Guide. https://www.indeed.com/career-advice/career-development/achieving-goals-quotes

101 Inspiring Mental Health Quotes. (2020, March 18). Mental Health Match. https://mentalhealthmatch.com/articles/anxiety/inspiring-mental-health-quotes

Adult Attention-Deficit/Hyperactivity Disorder (ADHD) - Symptoms and Causes. (2019, June 22). Mayo Clinic. https://www.mayoclinic.org/diseases-conditions/adult-adhd/symptoms-causes/syc-20350878

Bertino, K. (2021, May 24). *9 Tips for Creating a Routine for Adults with ADHD.* Psych Central. https://psychcentral.com/adhd/9-tips-for-creating-a-routine-for-adults-with-adhd#:~:text=If%20you%20have%20ADHD%2C%20creating

Chrissy. (2022, April 23). *21 Inspirational Daily Routine Quotes.* Organise My House. https://organisemyhouse.com/inspirational-daily-routine-quotes/

References

Danaher, M. (2022, September 27). *Positive Powerful Affirmations That Will Change Your Life*. Linkedin. https://www.linkedin.com/pulse/positive-powerful-affirmations-change-your-life-mark/

Danielson, M. L., Bitsko, R. H., Ghandour, R. M., Holbrook, J. R., Kogan, M. D., & Blumberg, S. J. (2018). Prevalence of Parent-Reported ADHD Diagnosis and Associated Treatment Among U.S. Children and Adolescents, 2016. *Journal of Clinical Child & Adolescent Psychology, 47*(2), 199–212. https://doi.org/10.1080/15374416.2017.1417860

Eddings, M. (2023). *Tilly in Technicolor*. Wednesday Books.

First Steps to Building Habits for Success. (n.d.). CHADD. Retrieved June 27, 2023, from https://chadd.org/adhd-weekly/first-steps-to-building-habits-for-success/#:~:text=Creating%20habits%20for%20success

Habits That Serve You Are Key to Success When You Have ADHD. (n.d.). CHADD. Retrieved June 27, 2023, from https://chadd.org/adhd-news/adhd-news-adults/habits-that-serve-you-are-key-to-success-when-you-have-adhd/#:~:text=Therefore%2C%20routine%20becomes%20an%20%20important

Honos-Webb, L. (2021, July 9). 6 Secrets to Goal Setting with ADHD. *ADDitude*. https://www.additudemag.com/achieving-personal-goals-adhd/#:~:text=Setting%20and%20achieving%20goals%20incre ases

How Does ADHD Affect Our Personal Hygiene and Routines. (2022, December 19). Www.theminiadhdcoach.com. https://www.theminiadhdcoach.com/living-with-adhd/adhd-and-personal-hygiene

How to make a morning routine with ADHD (and why you should). (n.d.). Inflow. Retrieved June 30, 2023, from https://www.getinflow.io/post/how-to-create-perfect-adhd-morning-routine

Jaksa, P. (2019, August 20). *The Importance of a Daily Schedule for Kids with ADHD*. ADHD Ireland. https://adhdireland.ie/the-importance-of-a-daily-schedule-for-kids-with-adhd-back-to-school-series/#:~:text=Children%20with%20ADHD%20need%20routine

Johnson, N. (2023). *Men with ADHD*.

Laoyan, S. (2022, August 4). *Overcome analysis paralysis with these 4 tips*. Asana. https://asana.com/resources/analysis-paralysis

Miller, G. (2013, January 12). *Meeting Your Goals When You Have ADHD: 9 Helpful Tips*. Psych Central. https://psychcentral.com/adhd/meeting-your-goals-when-you-have-adhd#:~:text=Goal%20setting%20when%20you%20have

Mink, M. (2017, July 30). *5 Ways To Create A Supportive Environment To Achieve Your Goals*. Driven Woman. https://driven-woman.com/blog/archive/5-ways-to-create-a-supportive-environment-to-achieve-your-goals/

Muinos, L. (2012, July 19). *ADHD Struggles: 8 Obstacles and How to Overcome Them*. Psych Central. https://psychcentral.com/adhd/adhd-struggles-coping-tips#recap

Parekh, R. (2017). *What Is ADHD?* American Psychiatric Association. https://www.psychiatry.org/patients-families/adhd/what-is-adhd

Quinn, P. O., & Madhoo, M. (2014). A Review of Attention-Deficit/Hyperactivity Disorder in Women and Girls. *The Primary Care Companion for CNS Disorders*, *16*(3). https://doi.org/10.4088/pcc.13r01596

Saline, S. (2023, January 9). *How to Stick to a Routine: Daily Routine Troubleshooting for ADHD Brains*. Additude Magazine. https://www.additudemag.com/how-to-stick-to-a-routine-adhd/

References

Scroggs, L. (n.d.). *The complete guide to time blocking.* Todoist. Retrieved July 10, 2023, from https://todoist.com/productivity-methods/time-blocking

Sheldon, R. (2022, September). *What is Pomodoro Technique time management?* What Is. https://www.techtarget.com/whatis/definition/pomodoro-technique#:~:text=The%20Pomodoro%20Technique%20is%20a

Silny, J. (2021, September 16). *Positive Affirmations for Success with ADHD.* ADDitude. https://www.additudemag.com/slideshows/positive-affirmations-for-success-with-adhd/

Simon, V., Czobor, P., Bálint, S., Mészáros, Á., & Bitter, I. (2009). Prevalence and correlates of adult attention-deficit hyperactivity disorder: meta-analysis. *British Journal of Psychiatry, 194*(3), 204–211. https://doi.org/10.1192/bjp.bp.107.048827

The Science of ADHD. (2018). CHADD. https://chadd.org/about-adhd/the-science-of-adhd/

Thomas, L. (2017, August 18). *How does ADHD Affect the Brain?* News-Medical.net. https://www.news-medical.net/health/How-does-ADHD-Affect-the-Brain.aspx#:~:text=ADHD%20is%20associated%20with%20abnormally

What Is ADHD? (2022, August 9). Centers for Disease Control and Prevention. https://www.cdc.gov/ncbddd/adhd/facts.html

Made in United States
North Haven, CT
03 February 2024